CREATION SINGS

40 Days of
Spiritual Wisdom
from the
Non-Human World

CREATION SINGS

40 Days of Spiritual Wisdom
from the Non-Human World

BRUCE G. EPPERLY

Anamchara
Books

© Bruce G. Epperly 2025

Anamchara Books
Vestal, New York 13850
www.AnamcharaBooks.com

All rights reserved. No part of this publication may be reproduced or transmitted for commercial purposes, except for brief quotations, without written permission of the publisher. Churches and other noncommercial interests may reproduce portions of this book without the express written permission of Anamchara Books, provided that the text does not exceed 500 words or 5 percent of the entire book, whichever is less, and that the text is not material quoted from another publisher. When reproducing text from this book, include the following credit line: "From *Creation Sings: Forty Days of Spiritual Wisdom from the Non-Human World* by Bruce G. Epperly, published by Anamchara Books. Used by permission."

Paperback ISBN: 978-1-62524-929-6
eBook ISBN: 978-1-62524-930-2

Dedicated to
my grandsons Jack and James
and all the children and youth of the world
and the companion animals that have given me love
and taught me the meaning of unconditional care:
our companion dogs Duke, Ed, Flaca,
Freddie, Chelsea, and Tucker, and our
companion cats, Charlie and Mr. Sweets.

Thank you! Thank you! Thank you!

Truly all dogs and cats—and pangolins and right whales—
go to heaven!

CONTENTS

Introduction: *Nature as the Body of God*	11
Day 1: *Consider the Lilies*	37
Day 2: *Bless the World*	41
Day 3: *Forever Young*	45
Day 4: *Persistence*	49
Day 5: *The Power of Positive Focus*	51
Day 6: *Obstacles to Spiritual Adventure*	55
Day 7: *The Peaceable Realm*	59
Day 8: *Preparation and Delight*	63
Day 9: *Home for the Restless Spirit*	65
Day 10: *Holy Friendship*	67
Day 11: *Living Beautifully*	71
Day 12: *Let It Shine*	73
Day 13: *Hope in the Unseen*	75

Day 14: *Don't Be Afraid* 77

Day 15: *Born to Sing* 79

Day 16: *Running the Race, One Step at a Time* 81

Day 17: *Welcoming Strangers* 83

Day 18: *Love Heals* 85

Day 19: *Now Is the Only Moment There Is* 87

Day 20: *A Place to Call Home and a Person to Love* 89

Day 21: *I See You* 91

Day 22: *World-Changing Faith* 93

Day 23: *Pure Joy* 95

Day 24: *The Passionate Life* 97

Day 25: *The Healing Power of Companionship* 99

Day 26: *A Sensational Life* 101

Day 27: *Rise Up!* 103

Day 28: *Listen as Well as Speak* 105

Day 29: *Rise and Shine*	107
Day 30: *For God's Sake, Use Your Brain!*	109
Day 31: *Strength in Stillness*	111
Day 32: *Everyone Matters*	113
Day 33: *Deep Intuition*	115
Day 34: *The Race Is to the Slow*	117
Day 35: *Breathe Deeply and Rest in God*	119
Day 36: *Healing Spirit*	121
Day 37: *Elephant Whisperers*	123
Day 38: *Touch Transforms*	125
Day 39: *Tasting and Smelling the Goodness of Creation*	127
Day 40: *The Phoenix*	129
Conclusion: *The Pilgrimage Continues: Running with the Elephants*	131

INTRODUCTION

Nature as the Body of God

Within the chaos of our lives, there is another melody—a symphony inspired by the persistent movements of the moral and spiritual arcs of history and evolutionary adventure, hailing the far-off dream of God's vision of truth, beauty, and goodness.

A World of Praise

We live in a world of praise. We live in a world of beauty and passion. Tragedy abounds, and yet beneath and within the pain and suffering—often inflicted by humankind upon one another and upon the non-human world—"there lives the dearest freshness deep down things." For all the damage humans have done to the world, the poet Gerard Manley Hopkins affirms that "Nature is never spent," and that there will be a graceful morning when the "Holy Ghost over the bent World broods with warm breast and with ah! bright wings."

Nature persists, despite human waywardness. Resilient and innovative, Nature moves forward with the energy of Creative Love—even as humankind attempts to divorce ourselves from the Nature on which we depend and of which we are a part.

Deep down, we are Nature. Nature gives birth to us as a species and sustains and empowers us in each moment of our lives. We are kin to the krill, kangaroos, fireflies, and pangolin. The ancients knew this. So do our toddler children and grandchildren, who rejoice in the Good Earth, still "trailing clouds of glory."

Psalm 148 charts a world of praise. Nature is alive—not just human nature or our companion animals, but the trees and flowers, the winds and snow. Even "the stars pray," as theologian and spiritual guide Jay McDaniel asserts. Long before materialistic philosophers and scientists—or anthropocentric theologians—imagined a lifeless world, reduced to matter in motion and fully malleable to human artifice, the psalmist and their companions among the First Americans, African sages, Indigenous peoples, and Celtic adventurers experienced "thin places" everywhere. They believed that all Creation is a theophany—transparent to God and revealing Holiness. "The heavens are telling the glory of God" (Psalm 19:1), and so are the cells of our bodies and the lilies of the field. A ladder of angels marks out every plot of land, and those with open senses proclaim with awestruck Jacob, "Surely God is in this place—and I did not know it!" This place is every place: right where you are, and in every creature you encounter.

As a child, I lived in a world of praise. Perhaps you lived in a lively, praising world as well. Pious from the very beginning of my life, I experienced a Reality for which I had no name—in the flowing waters of the Salinas River, the rooster crowing at daybreak, the running of my dog Duke, and the smog-free, star-filled heavens above. God routinely whispered to me in the breeze and the symphonies of sunrise chirping. I felt a kinship with all things and truly lived in the world of a song I learned in childhood. I felt the energy of God in the cracking of a ball on my baseball bat, God's breath in running the bases, and God's touch in the feel of the grass beneath my feet. Raised with a sense that God was as near as my next breath and my dog's wagging tail, I sang with gratitude:

> *This is my Father's world,*
> *And to my list'ning ears*

All Nature sings, and round me rings
The music of the spheres…
[God] shines in all that's fair;
In the rustling grass I hear Him pass,
He speaks to me everywhere.

Rabbi Abraham Joshua Heschel proclaims that radical amazement is at the heart of religious experience—and the great Jewish mystic and social activist is right. Long before they were stifled by lifeless dogma and authoritarian institutions, the great religions had their origins in mystical experiences that joined heaven and earth and illuminated the world of the senses, making every place a holy place and every person a reflection of God's face.

Now, in my Medicare years with a more spacious schedule, I am reclaiming the wonder and astonishment of my childhood. I am pausing and noticing and being transfixed by what I once believed to be ordinary and unexceptional things: my goldendoodle racing across the commons in our Potomac, Maryland, townhouse community; the full moon scudding across the clouds on my predawn walk; the touch of my fingers tapping on my computer keyboard; the texture of my grandson's hair; the aroma of a neighbor's pungent, garlicky dinner; and even the stiffness of my aging knees as I awaken each morning, remembering to join Creation in praising that "this is the day that God has made, and I will rejoice and be glad in it." With each step, I am reclaiming Abraham Joshua Heschel's exclamation after marching in Selma with Martin Luther King Jr.: "I felt like my legs were praying."

"Let everything that breathes praise God!" exclaims the psalmist. The world is permeated with Divinity. Life is luminous with revelation. There are, as the Celtic spiritual guides proclaimed, "thin places everywhere."

Perhaps two thousand years after Psalm 148 was first chanted, a pilgrim from Assisi perceived holiness in swallows and salmon, worms and fiery sparks, untamed wolves and persons with leprosy, and all those scorned and feared by the healthy and righteous. In the waning days of his life, Francis experienced the Energy of Love flowing through his body despite pain, debilitation, and impending death:

Be praised, my Lord, through all your creatures,
especially through my lord Brother Sun,
who brings the day; and you give light through him.
And he is beautiful and radiant in all his splendor!
Of you, Most High, he bears the likeness.
Praise be You, my Lord, through Sister Moon

*and the stars, in heaven you formed them
clear and precious and beautiful.
Praised be You, my Lord, through Brother Wind,
and through the air, cloudy and serene,
and every kind of weather through which
You give sustenance to Your creatures.
Praised be You, my Lord, through Sister Water,
which is very useful and humble and precious and chaste.
Praised be You, my Lord, through Brother Fire,
through whom you light the night, and he is beautiful
and playful and robust and strong.
Praised be You, my Lord, through Sister Mother Earth,
who sustains us and governs us and who produces
varied fruits with colored flowers and herbs.*

Francis could face his own mortality, knowing that within his life flowed God's Fountain of Love—energizing, illuminating, and empowering all Creation. This fountain inspired him to face death knowing that the One who gave the sparrows their hymns would also give him a word of praise that death could not silence. How can we keep from singing, when we live in a world of praise and revelation?

"This is my Father's world." While we might expand the hymn to embrace parents of all kinds and the wondrous diversity and fluidity of gender, those words I learned as a child still invite world-weary, anxious, and technologically overwhelmed persons to embrace a world of praise—where the creatures of Earth, sky, and sea; aboveground and underground; flying, walking, creeping, and swimming; and the circuits of the heavens above and the firmness beneath all reflect God's glory and teach us to embrace the Good Earth as our Mother and Home, the place of our beginnings and endings.

Despite our attempts to create a world of our own—unrelated and independent from our natural surroundings—we are embedded in the cycles of Nature and depend on creatures we seldom give heed to: krill, bees, and worms. The ancients and Indigenous people, as well as the Celtic sages, saw the non-human world as the teacher of humankind. Humans were guided by spirit animals. The creatures of Earth taught us virtues to live by. The non-human world was an icon, a window, a portal into seeing God's face everywhere. The lilies of the field, the color purple, and the birds of the air showed humans how to live gracefully and gratefully—and how to trust that in all things, God is faithful. God's providence is giving birth to the world around us and providing sustenance moment by moment. Blessed by God's abundant and nurturing revelation in sea, sky, and Earth, "all we have needed Thy hand hath provided."

Reclaiming a world of praise, recovering our sense of unity with the non-human world, and embracing the creaturely world as kin is the pathway to our survival and flourishing in an age threatened by global climate change, environmental collapse, desecration of sacred spaces, and human violence and incivility. In reclaiming a sense of reverence for life on its own terms—not as an object of human manipulation and artifice—we rediscover the holiness of our lives, the sacredness of human diversity, and our absolute dependence on the graces of the non-human world and the One who parents all Creation.

We join with Creation in praise and partnership. Let heaven and Nature sing, and let humankind and all creatures of this Good Earth praise God.

Graceful Interdependence

The apostle Paul understood the interconnection of life. "If one member suffers," he writes, "all suffer together with it; if one member is honored, all rejoice together with it. Now you are the body of Christ and individually members of it" (1 Corinthians 12:26–27). Martin Luther King Jr. spoke to the same reality, saying, "We are caught in an inescapable network of mutuality, tied into a single garment of destiny.

Whatever affects one directly affects all indirectly. We are made to live together because of the interrelated structure of reality." On another occasion, he said, "I cannot be what I ought to be until you are what you ought to be. And you can never be what you ought to be until I am what I ought to me. That's the way God's universe is made."

We are connected. A butterfly flapping its wings in Pacific Grove, California, shapes weather patterns in Washington, D.C. A solar flare 93 million miles from Earth disrupts satellite communications. Toxins in the drinking water of Flint, Michigan, cause childhood illness and awaken protest. The health of plankton in the ocean contributes to sea life survival and air quality, inspiring a high school girl to rise in global activism. The world is one vast, intricate ecosystem. Gaia, the Great Earth Mother of the human and non-human world, flows in us and through us—and her health is the foundation of our own wellbeing. "One cannot pluck a flower without stirring a star," said Francis Thompson. The whole universe conspires to create each moment of experience. Our lives and decisions shape the unfolding future of Earth and all her creatures.

The Earth, as Martin Luther King Jr. once noted, is a neighborhood. It is up to us to make it a kinship, a family in which all beings, in their diversity, are cherished not only for how they serve human interests but also for their own intrinsic value.

We are connected. Every part of us is connected to the whole universe—to the cells in our bodies and to the first burst of energy that birthed this cosmos. We are not alone or adrift. We are part of an intricate, dynamic, and evolving universe, shaping and being shaped in turn.

One of my favorite moments in literature comes from Thornton Wilder's *Our Town*, in which a letter is addressed to:

> *Jane Crofut*
> *The Crofut Farm*
> *Grover's Corners*
> *Sutton County*
> *New Hampshire*
> *The United States of America*
> *North America*
> *The Earth*
> *The Solar System;*
> *The Universe*
> *The Mind of God*

Even in ordinary experience, we can never find a truly isolated individual or species. The boundary between self and world is nearly nonexistent. As I sit in the predawn hours writing this, my mind, my fingers, and the keyboard are one. I'm one with the arts-and-crafts chair I sit on and the multicolored afghan draped across my knees this cold winter morning.

My goldendoodle, Tucker—ninety-five pounds of fur and affection—has padded in to join me. A streetlight across the parking lot of our townhouse community glows softly. A newsfeed on my phone brings word of political leaders tied to white nationalism and efforts to erode American democracy. The smell of coffee drifts in from the kitchen. My first sip warms me. This is a thin place: a quiet, Spirit-soaked moment that gives birth to the words you're now reading—words that join us across miles, as if we were sitting side by side.

My microcosmic experience in suburban Maryland flows into and from the macrocosm of air, sea, sky, and Earth—not to mention international politics and planetary ecology. Deep down, I am one with the child yearning for breakfast in Gaza, the mourners in Israel, the Sudanese refugee, the young family in a Central American caravan, the MAGA protester afraid of change, and the whale gliding beneath warming seas. I am because you are. We are because of one another.

I am unique—but not separate. My story is part of a wondrous, fluid, diverse, and dynamic web of interconnection. There is no true "other" in this universe.

Theologians and scientists alike speak of the anthropic principle: the idea that life depends on a narrow band of physical conditions. Without the exact right mix of oxygen, carbon, gravity, and radiation, life on Earth could not exist. But this truth applies not just to humans—it applies to bees, plankton, whales, cats, swallows. Every creature is the result of billions of years of cosmic, galactic, solar, and planetary evolution, shaped by Divine providence moving through competition and community, accident and intention.

As Psalm 8 puts it, we are "a little lower than the angels"—but still carbon-based, Earth-born beings. Our Divinity is continuous with the Divine Spirit filling all Creation. When we open our eyes to this mystery, awe arises naturally. Gratitude follows. Dag Hammarskjöld, the mystic and U.N. Secretary-General, said it best:

> *For all that has been—thanks!*
> *For all that shall be—yes!*

That yes—our "yes" to Creation—shapes what shall be. It calls us into reverence and responsibility. It urges us to live in gratitude for our planetary kin and to act on behalf of future generations.

Environmentalist Bill McKibben once said that the best thing an individual can do for the climate is to stop being an individual. We must claim our place within a shared planetary destiny.

Life is always changing. Behold: God is always doing a new thing. God's mercies are new every morning. The God who centers us also centers all of Creation—moving through every atom, every galaxy, joining individuality with community, and laboring to heal our divisions with one another and with the more-than-human world.

We often imagine trees as self-contained: drawing from soil, rain, and sunlight with indifference to their neighbors. But science—and perhaps the Spirit—tells a different story. Trees, says Peter Wohlleben, are connected through their roots, forming a living network underground. Once connected, "they have no choice but to exchange nutrients." A beech forest thrives not in isolation, but through cooperation. When trees grow closely together, nutrients and water are shared, enabling each to grow into the best tree it can be.

When we remove some trees to "help" the others by eliminating competition, we actually do harm. The remaining trees lose their network. The forest becomes exposed. Harsh sunlight and swirling winds disrupt the moist, shaded floor. The well-being of the trees depends on the well-being of the whole.

Wohlleben's vision of the forest echoes Paul's vision of the Body of Christ:

> *If one member suffers, all suffer together.*
> *If one is honored, all rejoice together.*
> (1 Corinthians 12:26)

Could it be that Earth itself is the Body of Christ writ large? That the mycelial networks beneath our feet are teaching us how to live in harmony again?

Could the forest—silent, breathing, radiant—be a prophet?

Could Gaia, the Great Mother, be healed when we do something beautiful not only for God but for Earth?

Healing the World

The Prophet Isaiah had a vision of what a healed world would look like:

> The wolf will live with the lamb, the leopard will lie down with the goat, the calf and the lion and the yearling together; and a little child will lead

them. The cow will feed with the bear, their young will lie down together, and the lion will eat straw like the ox. The infant will play near the cobra's den, and the young child will put its hand into the viper's nest. They will neither harm nor destroy on all my holy mountain, for the earth will be filled with the knowledge of Yahweh as the waters cover the sea. (Isaiah 11:6–9)

Centuries later, Paul, the follower of the Christ, also writes about a healed Earth: "For the creation waits with eager longing for the revealing of the children of God . . . the creation itself will be set free from its enslavement to decay and will obtain the freedom of the glory of the children of God" (Romans 8: 22,24). God yearns and works to heal our world.

Alongside *"Jesus wept"* (John 11:35), the first biblical verse I ever memorized was John 3:16: *"For God so loved the world that he gave his only Son, so that everyone who believes in him may not perish but may have eternal life."* In my childhood spiritual formation, this verse served as an invitation to "accept Jesus as your personal savior." I was told: *"See how much God loves you? Jesus died for you, and you need to accept God's gift of salvation."*

Only later did I learn that the original Greek says, *"God so loved the cosmos."* Not just humanity—God loved all reality. God's fountain of love flows into all of Creation: the wind and rain, the caterpillar becoming butterfly, the soaring eagle and crashing waves, the chickens in our backyard, the riot of color in Creation—and humanity in all its diversity.

These days, many people use the word *deconstruction* to describe the painful process of outgrowing a vision of God that has become too small, exclusive, or violent. If your spirituality begins to stifle your spirit, something has to give. You either jettison that faith—or you wither inside it.

A humorous but tragic story marks my own first moment of deconstruction. At five or six years old, I already sensed God's love in all Creation. I was especially drawn to dogs, though our family didn't yet have one. One weekend, my parents went to a Baptist convention and left us with a pious woman named Mrs. Orr. She had a playful little dog—possibly a poodle—named Taffy. All weekend, Taffy and I were inseparable. It was boy meets dog, and boy falls in love.

Toward the end of the weekend, still brimming with childhood mysticism and evangelical piety, I asked Mrs. Orr, "Will Taffy go to heaven?"

She paused, visibly annoyed. Then, as if I'd broken a precious piece of china, she said curtly, "You better talk to your father. He'll set you straight. Jesus didn't die for animals."

Her answer shocked me. *God doesn't love Taffy?* I couldn't say it then, but I knew in my bones that she was wrong. Even at that age, something in me understood what the Celtic theologian Pelagius taught centuries earlier: every child enters the world bearing the image of God—not bearing inherited sin—and I was sure the same was true of dogs.

Taffy loved me. I loved Taffy. And in one tender weekend, that little dog showed me an image of unconditional love that still shapes who I'm trying to become. Inspired by my childlike sense of Divine presence, I used to walk through our neighborhood chanting: *"Jesus loves the little children, all the children of the world,"* and I'd add my own verse: *"Jesus loves the little critters, all the critters of the world."*

Saint Francis of Assisi received his vocation in the Chapel of San Damiano. As he prayed before a crucifix, he heard the words: *Repair my church, which has fallen into disrepair.* At first, he thought God meant the crumbling building itself. But gradually, he realized the message went deeper: God was calling him to heal a materialistic, crusading, power-hungry Church—to change its values, and help it remember who and what it was meant to be.

Later, Francis came to see that God's voice spoke not just through scripture but through all Creation. Every creature is part of the sacred story. All deserve our reverence and ethical consideration.

A similar concept appears in Jewish mysticism: *tikkun olam*, the calling to *"repair the world."* We are meant to be co-laborers with God in healing Creation—joining the broken pieces of existence and restoring the cosmos to wholeness.

Pause for a moment. Let these words settle:

Our calling is to be God's companions in healing the Earth.

We are healers—not of a world that was ever perfect but of a world that is good and growing. Rabbi White, a dear friend of mine, once reminded me that in Genesis, God calls Creation *"good"* and *"very good"*—but never *"perfect."* Perfection leaves no room for growth. But goodness allows for change, novelty, adventure—and healing.

We're not the only healers. Our non-human kin heal, too. Their presence teaches us how to live with trust and grace. One of my friends is accompanied everywhere by her service dog, who calms her spirit and helps her navigate daily life. Another friend once told me that the morning birdsong in her neighborhood reminds her to wake up praising God rather than worrying about the day ahead.

I often pray Isaiah 40:31 with those facing illness or grief. It's a prayer that joins us to the soaring eagle and the strength of our own bodies:

Those who wait for the Lord shall renew their strength;
They shall mount up with wings like eagles,
They shall run and not be weary;
They shall walk and not faint. (Isaiah 40:31)

Paleontologist and mystic Pierre Teilhard de Chardin once said we need a "new Francis" for the modern world. I believe our collective calling is to become that Francis. Each of us is invited to embody the spirit of the twelfth-century saint—and to listen to the voice of the twenty-first-century one, Pope Francis, whose encyclical *Laudato Si'* calls us to cooperate *"as instruments of God for the care of creation, each according to his or her own culture, experience, involvement, and talents."*

Theodore Parker, a Unitarian minister, once reflected on the moral arc of history in words later paraphrased by Martin Luther King Jr.: "I do not pretend to understand the moral universe; the arc is a long one. . . . Our eyes reach but little ways. . . . But from what we can see, we are sure it bends toward justice."

We do not stand apart from Nature; we are part of Nature. And our healing depends on the healing of the Earth. We join hands—human and non-human—in a song of planetary healing. We march toward eco-justice. We become companions to all Creation, faithful to our God, our planet, and all who dwell on this Earth.

Wisdom from the Non-Human World

When Jesus talked to his followers during his time on Earth, he often used stories and metaphors from the non-human world. "Consider the lilies of the field, how they grow; they neither toil nor spin, yet I tell you, even Solomon in all his glory was not clothed like one of these. But if God so clothes the grass of the field, which is alive today and tomorrow is thrown into the oven, will he not much more clothe you—you of little faith?. . . So do not worry about tomorrow, for tomorrow will bring worries of its own. Today's trouble is enough for today" (Matthew 6:28–30, 34).

Creation sings! Creation also teaches and inspires! Creation heals and transforms! The heavens declare God's glory and all creatures of God sing "alleluia." For those whose senses are awakened and purified the world is both infinite and intimate. As the Hindu sages proclaim, the world is *lila,* the divine play of God, inviting us to play and rejoice with all our earthly kin. Although the animistic vision of Creation as a living reality was dismissed by adherents of the modern world view as superstitious, unscientific, and primitive compared to their "sophisticated" materialistic understanding of reality, scientists and spiritual guides alike are rediscovering an enchanted universe, or as my human teacher and mentor David Ray Griffin says a "reenchanted" universe in which we integrate high tech and high touch, CT scans with radical amazement at the wonders of our physical bodies, and satellite technology with delight in leaping dolphins and the migration of monarch butterflies. After once exorcising the spirit from the non-human world, scientists and theologians are now rediscovering a very different vision of the world: a living universe in which mind, body, and spirit are intricately connected, the environment shapes human health and well-being, and "all nature sings and around me rings the music of the spheres." Instead of interpreting human existence in terms of mechanical cause and effect, conditioning, and firing neurons, many scientists have found that it is more accurate to recognize that the consciousness and creativity we see in ourselves is present everywhere, in varying degrees, in the universe. Crows solve puzzles. Humpbacked whales sing melodies. Elephants mourn for life. Dogs detect cancer cells and calm anxious children. Trees send signals to their peers and flowers reach out to bees, and putting us humans to shame, gray wolves, swans, coyotes, angel fish, and shingleback lizards mate for life.

We live in an intelligent and wisely guided universe. There is chance, accident, competition, earthquake, tsunami, violence, war, and incivility. Yet, the moral, spiritual, and evolutionary love of God flows and inspires wholeness and growth through all the accidents and conflicts of life If, as theologians assert, God is omnipresent, then God is revealed directly or indirectly in every creature and each encounter. Divine wisdom comes to us from the orderly movements of the heavens and our relationships with our companion animals. Wise spiritual teachers remind us to consider the lilies, take heed of the ant, and delight along with breaching whales and leaping dolphins. Remember again the poetic vision of a living, God-filled universe, described by Maltbie Babcock. This is the "real" world, not the world of dead matter, insentient creatures, isolated individualism, and valueless nature.

All nature sings, and round me rings
The music of the spheres.
This is my Father's world:
I rest me in the thought
Of rocks and trees, of skies and seas—
His hand the wonders wrought...
God speaks to me everywhere.

Even the stones cry out to speak God's truth to us, as Jesus says (Luke 19:40). We can learn something from the rock of ages as well as the age of rocks! That's the heart of the adventure we are about to begin. God is speaking to us through the experiences of the non-human world and the example of the order and novelty of Nature. If we train our senses, we will glimpse God's wisdom in sparrows, lilies, the color purple, and mother hens as well as in our relationships with our companion animals and our own dreams, intuitions, insights, and moments of transcendence. We will discover holiness in the rock of ages in the rocks upon which we stand.

In the forty days ahead, I invite you to pause and notice and then be transformed by the daily spiritual messages and the world around you. There are many ways to approach the next forty days. In the process of writing this book, my writing became a central spiritual practice. I first contemplated the theme of the day and considered the spiritual witness of the non-human world. Then, I put on my walking shoes and headed out for a predawn walk in my Potomac, Maryland, neighborhood, pondering the message of the day as well as simply letting my senses graze and be nourished by the world around me. I returned home and jotted down any insights I had, joining my vocation as a writer and my lived experience of beauty.

If walking presents a problem, due to mobility issues, weather, or environment, I invite you simply to gaze out your window. Even urban environments can reveal God's quest for beauty and invitation to amazement. Creation speaks to us wherever we are.

As we go forth on this holy adventure with the non-human world, I invite you on a spiritual pilgrimage, whether in movement or meditative stability, with the words of a Navajo blessing.

In beauty I walk,
With beauty before me I walk,
With beauty behind me I walk,
With beauty above me I walk,
With beauty around me I walk...
I walk with beauty around me.
My words will be beautiful.
In beauty all day long may I walk.
Through the returning seasons, may I walk.
On the trail marked with pollen may I walk.
With dew about my feet, may I walk.
With beauty before me may I walk.
With beauty behind me may I walk.
With beauty below me may I walk.
With beauty above me may I walk.
With beauty all around me may I walk.
Wandering on a trail of beauty, lively, may I walk.
Wandering on a trail of beauty,
living again, may I walk.
My words will be beautiful. . . .
It has become beauty again.

DAY 1
Consider the Lilies

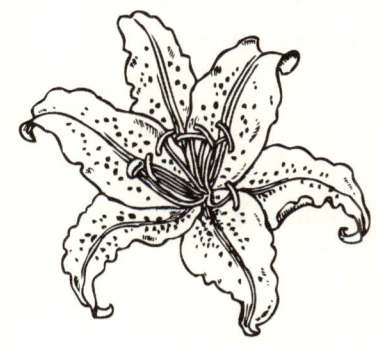

Consider the lilies
of the field,
how they grow; they
neither toil nor spin,
yet I tell you, even
Solomon in all his glory
was not clothed
like one of these.
But if God so clothes the grass of the field,
which is alive today and tomorrow
is thrown into the oven,
will God not much more clothe you. . . .
So do not worry about tomorrow.

Matthew 6:28–30, 34

The life of a lily is brief. From bud "break" to full blossom is seldom more than two weeks. Fragile and precarious, lilies burst forth in all their glory, shouting to Creation,

"Look at me. Wake up. In this brief moment, I'm beautiful. That is enough." In their brief moment of life, they live fully. Deep down, lilies know that they are achieving their vocation simply by letting their beauty burst forth. They don't put off to tomorrow what God calls them to do today. They embrace the luminosity of the moment, inspiring delight and adding beauty to the world. If we live this moment and this life with the joy we see in the lilies and other blossoms, heaven will surely take care of itself!

While we may disregard the lilies of the field, God blesses them with beauty beyond the finest fashion designs. If God cares for the lilies, won't God care for you? Won't God delight in your gifts and rejoice when you burst forth in beauty and service?

Our lives are brief and fragile in the fourteen-billion-year journey of the universe. Our individual lives appear of little significance among the billions of human and non-human kin living on Earth. And yet, we matter. This moment matters. God births us forth with the same love that God brought forth the Big Bang of the Universe, the lilies of the field, and the birds of the air. Awakened to God's intimate and loving care, let your beauty shine and, as Mother (Saint) Teresa counsels, "do something beautiful for God" and be something beautiful for God.

*Awaken me to this one shining moment of life
that I might live fully, love greatly,
and bring beauty to this Good Earth
and all my human and non-human kin.*

DAY 2
Bless the World

Love your enemies and pray
for those who persecute you,
so that you may be children
of your Parent in heaven,
for he makes his sun rise
on the evil and on the good
and sends rain on the righteous
and on the unrighteous. . . .
Be perfect as your Heavenly Parent is perfect.

Matthew 5:44–45

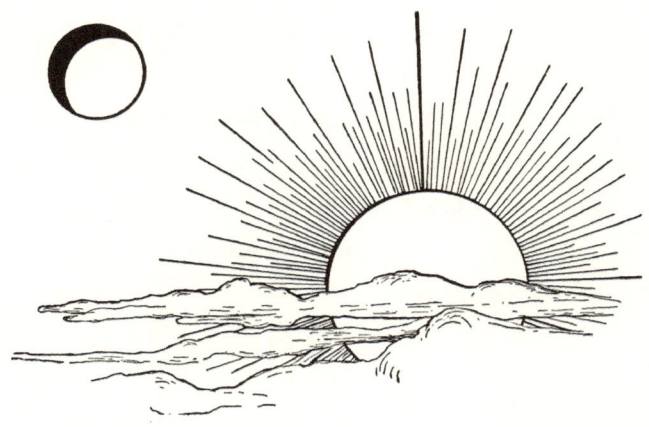

Creation sings! Creation shines! Creation rains! All things gleam! The world is renewed and refreshed by sun and sky. The sun shines and the rains fall on everyone, friend and foe, without exception. Nature's bounty descends on companion and stranger. Asylum seekers heading to the U.S. borderlands and anti-immigrant protesters alike feel the warmth of the sun and the refreshment of rain. No child is denied the blessings of sunlight and rainfall or the changing seasons. Nature witnesses to God's perfect love that nurtures Creation in all its wondrous diversity. Like God, Nature blesses everyone, without exception.

Shine like the sun! Refresh like the wind! Be a light to the world! Where can you give light and life to the world? Where can you bathe a stranger with radiant and refreshing love? The perfection of God, and human fulfillment, reveals itself as a circle without circumference and a spirit without boundaries. Even when we must protest harmful public policies, challenge injustice, and ensure an orderly border and path to citizenship, we must welcome, embrace, and include all humankind and the non-human world as God's beloved kin. The wind and rain remind us that we all belong and that division is an illusion.

*Circle of Love, let my love be
as complete and perfect
as the shining sun and falling rain.
Expand my care for humankind
and the non-human world,
to see the well-being of others
as connected to my own well-being.
Let me, like the Creator,
be perfect in loving hospitality
for all God's Creation.*

DAY 3
Forever Young

Francis of Assisi was "always new, always fresh, always beginning again."

Thomas of Celeno, *The Life of St. Francis*

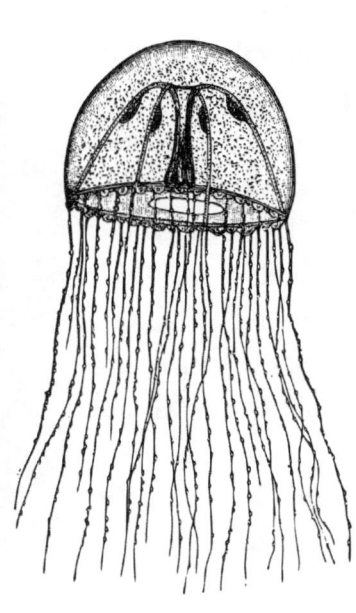

Even the smallest creatures can teach us something about our spiritual lives. Watching a *Wild Kratts* episode on PBS several years ago with my young grandchildren, I learned about "the immortal jellyfish." *Turritopsis dohrnii*, the immortal jellyfish, is a small jelly fish (about one-fifth of an inch in length and width) living in the waters of the Mediterranean Sea and off the coast of Japan. According to marine scientists, when a *T. dohrnii* jellyfish encounters environmental challenge, experiences stress, is threatened by physical attack, or becomes elderly or sick, its cells are transformed, and the jellyfish reverts back to its polyp or youthful state, giving birth to a new polyp colony. In theory, this reversal of the aging process can go on indefinitely, if not interfered with by predators, rendering members of this jellyfish species biologically immortal.

Under stress and challenge, we often freeze emotionally, intellectually, and spiritually. We revert to old ways of dealing with issues instead of boldly trying something new. We become intellectually brittle and politically inflexible. Aging and illness often diminish our imaginations as well as our physical well-being. The immortal jellyfish reminds us that external circumstances can be an invitation to novelty and freshness of spirit. The energy of love and creativity flows through us and we can access it at any time. Deep down, there is a part of us that is forever young. Indeed, as a song from *South Pacific* my mother played in my childhood noted, "younger than springtime are you." We can attempt new behaviors and entertain previously unimagined possibilities. We can initiate novelty to match and exceed the novelties that confront us. Behold! We can do a new thing. We can be creative under stress. We can choose to be "always new, always fresh, always beginning again."

*Spirit of Adventure,
awaken me to new possibilities,
and give me the courage to explore new paths
spiritually, intellectually, and relationally.
Let me take the risk of a novel behavior
or fresh ways to look at the world.
May my spirit always be willing to begin anew.*

DAY 4

Persistence

It always seems impossible until it's done.

Nelson Mandela

My Scots mother Loretta Baxter, of the MacMillan clan, often told me the story of Robert the Bruce and the spider. Because my name was "Bruce," I had an affinity with the Scottish king. Defeated by the English armies, Robert the Bruce hid in a cave, hopeless about the future and ready to give up the fight. As he languished in despair, he noticed a small spider attempting to weave a web. The spider tried and failed over and over. Each time the spider fell, it climbed back up to try again. Finally, the spider's silk took hold, and the spider managed to spin a web. In contemplating the spider's persistence, Robert the Bruce saw his struggles from a new perspective, realized the power of resilience, and was inspired to fight and defeat the English army against overwhelming odds.

"Never give in, never, never, never in nothing great or small, large or petty," challenged Winston Churchill during the dark days of World War II. The obstacles to spiritual growth and professional accomplishment can seem overwhelming. The odds often appear against our realizing our dreams or experiencing peace of mind. Yet, Gautama Buddha sat under the Bodhi tree, vowing not to leave until he experienced enlightenment. His persistence gave birth to a great religious movement. Like the spider, he persisted despite temptation, distraction, and weariness. One moment at a time, one hour at a time, one day at time, we can persist, overcoming failures, with our eyes on the prize of healing, wholeness, peace, and justice.

*Thank you for the spider's persistence
and the spirit of perseverance
you have implanted in my heart.
Despite obstacles and previous failures,
give me courage for the second wind,
the next effort, and one more push,
knowing that the God of tomorrow
and the faith of the future guide my steps.*

DAY 5

The Power of Positive Focus

Right mindfulness.

The Buddhist Nobel
Eightfold Path to Enlightenment

An unknown ninth-century Irish monk compares his own quest for self-awareness with his cat's keen focus on feline vocation. In observing his companion cat, he finds guidance for his own spiritual life.

I and Pangur Bán, my cat,
'Tis a like task we are at;
Hunting mice is his delight,
Hunting words I sit all night. . . .

Practice every day has made
Pangur perfect in his trade;
I get wisdom day and night
Turning darkness into light.

Right mindfulness and self-awareness are at the heart of spiritual growth: discovering your spiritual path, living intentionally, awakening to practices that support your quest for intimacy with God and your neighbor, and then mindfully focusing on what brings healing and wholeness to your life.

Pangur Bán focuses on hunting mice. He knows what brings him joy and then mindfully pursues it. Of course, Pangur enjoys other activities: playing with yarn and sitting on his companion's lap, stretching and capering around the house. But Pangur chooses to do one thing at a time. Fully immersed in the task at hand, he mindfully lives in the moment, fulfilling his vocation with delight and skill, reminding us to stay centered in our spirits as we respond to the many challenges of life.

*Wake me up to the wonder of this moment,
O God of Persistent Love. Keep me on track,
focusing on what gives me delight
and inspires growth
in body, mind, spirit, and community
with those around me and this Good Earth.
Like Pangur the cat, let me delight
in practicing my craft, deepening my spirit
and staying focused on my vocation
one moment at a time.*

DAY 6

Obstacles to Spiritual Adventure

Lord Ganesh of curved elephant trunk and huge body,
> Whose brilliance is equal to billions of suns in intensity,
> Always removes all obstacles from my endeavours truly,
> I respectfully pray to him with all my revered sincerity.

Munindra Misra,
Chants of Hindu Gods and Goddesses in English Rhyme

In Hindu spirituality, Ganesh (or Ganesha), known by his elephant head and four arms, is the god who removes obstacles in our spiritual journey, and sometimes places temporary obstacles in our way, like a coach or trainer, when we become too enamored of our own achievements. Ganesh is a hybrid in many ways, joining the strength of an elephant with the wisdom of a deity. Whenever they begin a new adventure or project, followers of Ganesh invoke the deity's power to provide a way where there is no way, break apparently insurmountable barriers, and encourage the successful completion of tasks that prosper our endeavors and promote our well-being and the well-being of others. Ganesh, who is also the patron of the arts and sciences, and spirit of wisdom and intellect, provides, like the earthly elephant, support in our quest to overcome life's obstacles.

The elephant reminds us that we have the power to face the obstacles of life with courage and wisdom. There is strength and wisdom within each one of us propelling us toward fulfilling the vocations God has given us. We can bend and push God's arc of justice forward with courage and perseverance, making a way through the jungles and challenges of our life and communities.

*God, give me the strength and wisdom
of Ganesh.
Give me power and wisdom
to face life's obstacles with courage
and persistence.
Help me to claim my role
in bending the moral arc of the universe
toward justice and peace.*

DAY 7

The Peaceable Realm

**Lord, make me an instrument of Your peace;
Where there is hatred, let me sow love;
Where there is injury, pardon.**

attributed to St. Francis

Francis's first followers told the story of a dangerous wolf who tormented the citizens of the Umbrian village of Gubbio, Italy. The fearful villagers sent hunters to kill the wolf, but the wolf eluded them and continued to terrorize the town, frightening children and killing livestock.

To the astonishment of the villagers, Francis went unarmed into the woods to confront the wolf. When the wolf saw him, it charged—but stopped in its tracks when Francis made the sign of the cross and chastised the creature for its violent behavior. Then Francis commanded the wolf to choose the path of peace and forbade it from attacking the townspeople and their animals.

He also instructed the villagers to welcome the wolf as a fellow citizen and ensure that it was fed and treated with respect. The wolf experienced a transformation of spirit—and a greater conversion occurred when the villagers embraced the wolf, forming a bond of mutual care, protection, and peace.

The legend of the wolf of Gubbio teaches us that even those filled with violence can change. We, too, can lay down our weapons, listen to the better angels of our nature, make peace with our enemies, and work for nonviolent solutions to global and personal problems. Francis saw the angel hidden in a vicious wolf—and then the wolf saw that holiness in himself.

Giver of Life,
make me an instrument of your peace,
sowing love and healing,
welcoming the stranger,
and seeing holiness even in those
whose politics or behavior offend me.
Help me to see angels in everyone,
including myself,
and out of that vision,
become a peacemaker in all my affairs.

DAY 8

Preparation and Delight

> Go to the ant, you sluggard;
> consider its ways and be wise!
> It has no commander,
> no overseer or ruler,
> yet it stores its provisions in summer
> and gathers its food at harvest.

Proverbs 6:6–8

One warm summer day, a grasshopper plays its fiddle in the sunshine while a nose-to-the-grindstone ant spends the day trudging back and forth, carrying supplies. The grasshopper delights in the moment, while the ant diligently prepares for the future. When winter comes, the ant is well-fed—but the grasshopper is not. When the grasshopper asks for food, the ant scolds him for being unprepared and turns him away.

This old fable is often told to highlight the virtues of hard work and preparation—and it's true that planning is important. We do need to prepare: for winter, for emergencies, for retirement. A wise person saves for a rainy day. But we must also make room for joy and generosity. Tough love without compassion is just toughness. And all work, without celebration, deadens the spirit.

Spiritual wholeness requires a dance between diligence and delight. Like the ant, we prepare. Like the grasshopper, we play. We plan for tomorrow, but we also meditate in the sunshine. We work hard—and we rejoice in the ordinary wonders of the day. Joy and planning, daydreaming and structure, faith and flexibility: these are the twin rhythms of a flourishing spiritual life.

Thank you, God of Changing Seasons,
for summer's warmth and winter's chill.
Guide me to rejoice in my work,
plan for the future with flexibility,
and find time to delight
in the beauty of this moment,
trusting your care through all the seasons of life.

DAY 9

Home for the Restless Spirit

> Our hearts are restless until they find their rest in you.
>
> Augustine of Hippo

Near my childhood home in the Salinas Valley is the Pacific Grove Monarch Butterfly Sanctuary. Each autumn, some 13,000 monarch butterflies return, guided by an inner GPS, to a grove of pine, sycamore, and cypress trees in this Pacific Ocean town. They cluster in trees to warm themselves, seek shelter, and feed in the sanctuary's garden.

Scientists still don't fully understand what draws monarchs back from Canada, the Rockies, and the northeastern United States each year to the same sites in Pacific Grove and Central Mexico. But the migration happens—faithfully, seasonally—an ancient rhythm embedded in their being.

We, too, are looking for a place to call home. Adult children return for the holidays. Travelers feel relief when the Uber rounds the corner and home comes into view. I love to travel—but my heart sings when I see our townhouse after a long trip. These moments echo the ancient truth expressed by the fourth-century North African saint: "God, you have made us for yourself, and our hearts are restless until they find their rest in you."

What is your heart yearning for? What is your true home? Do you have a sacred space in your house—or in Nature? Where do you rest in Spirit before heading into your next adventure?

Pilgrim God, like the monarch butterfly,
we are winging our way toward home.
Guide our steps and our choices,
that we might find our true home—
centered in you, O God,
and joined with all Creation
in the peace that passes understanding.
Calm our restless hearts
and energize us for the journey ahead.

DAY 10

Holy Friendship

> You shall love your neighbor as yourself.
>
> Mark 12:31

Dogs can truly be a human's best friend. A dog named Holly, for example, travels everywhere with Susan, a former student of mine who lives in the DC area. A veteran of the Afghan war, Susan suffers from post-traumatic stress disorder, which often manifests as anxiety and fear—especially in unfamiliar places and situations. Although she holds down a responsible job, she still feels insecure when she leaves home or goes on business trips.

"With Holly by my side," says Susan, "I feel safe and calm. She seems to know how I feel. She stands beside me or pushes her head against me, and then everything's all right. I don't know what I'd do without her. I have human companions who love me—I have two children and a wife. But Holly is my loyal traveling companion. Her silence quiets my spirit and eases my stress. She is an angel in disguise."

"Dog" is *God* spelled backwards. Or is "God" *dog* spelled backwards? In either case, our companion animals—especially service animals—are angels in our lives, messengers of God who calm our spirits and inspire the confidence to face life's challenges.

Holly is a spiritual teacher. She not only helps Susan find calm in novel situations, but she also reminds us that we, too, are called to be messengers of God for one another. Our vocation is to bring peace and wholeness into every situation, even amid conflict and stress, by making healing our goal. The prayer of Saint Francis pleads: "Lord, make me an instrument of peace." That peace brings calm, healing, empowerment, and reconciliation.

Let us be "service" persons and angels to one another—calming each other's spirits, comforting one another in anxiety, and providing both the spiritual and material support needed to flourish.

*Give me a loyal and loving spirit,
Companion God.
Let me feel your nearness
so that I might experience your calm presence—
and in response, bring peace to the storms
that surround me, enabling others
to know wholeness and safety,
even in difficult moments.*

DAY 11

Living Beautifully

With Beauty all around me I walk.

Navajo blessing

According to legend, during the Middle Ages European farms were plagued by pests. Farmers began praying to the Virgin Mary to save their crops. Soon, they began seeing helpful ladybugs in their fields, and the crops were miraculously spared. These red-and-black beetles came to be known as "our Lady's birds" or "lady beetles." German farmers called them *Marienkäfer*, or "Mary beetles."

The seven-spotted ladybug, a member of the beetle family, is believed to be the first insect named in honor of the Virgin Mary. Its red color represents her cloak; its black spots, her seven sorrows. As a tribute to their beauty, a group of ladybugs is poetically called a "loveliness."

Philosopher Alfred North Whitehead claimed that the aim of the universe is the production of beauty. In their protection of flowers and crops from pests, ladybugs teach us that beauty can be beneficial—for our well-being, and for the health of our gardens and communities.

Some spiritual teachers suggest that whenever you see a ladybug, you should give thanks for the beauty and blessings in your life. Gratitude, however, is not meant to foster passivity. From thankfulness springs action. Like the ladybug, we can be both beautiful and beneficial—inspiring others toward abundant life and protecting the vulnerable from harm.

Artist of Creation, thank you for beauty,
for the simple beauty of ladybugs—
and the beauty you've placed in me.
Let that beauty flow through me
to bring healing to the world.

DAY 12

Let It Shine

> This little light of mine,
> I'm gonna let it shine....
> Everywhere I go
> I'm gonna let it shine.
>
> African American spiritual

Every summer evening, I wait in anticipation for the first firefly of the season. Each year, fewer of these nocturnal beetles—also known as lightning bugs or glow worms—appear in our neighborhood. But when I spot that first flicker, my heart fills with joy. These fragile creatures are not only beautiful—they are a reminder of the power of even the smallest light to pierce the darkness.

Fireflies are little lights shining bravely in the dark. Jesus said, "The light shines in the darkness, and the darkness did not overtake it" (John 1:5). A single glimmer of light, even a fragile beam, can guide a pilgrim through the darkest night.

You can *see* the light—as poet Amanda Gorman says—and then *be* the light, giving guidance and inspiring beauty to those around you. Let your little light shine, wherever you are and wherever you go. You, like the firefly, are the light of the world.

*Today, I will light my world with beauty and love.
Let your Divine light shine through me,
growing ever brighter and piercing the darkness.*

DAY 13

Hope in the Unseen

**Now faith is the assurance
of things hoped for,
the conviction of things not seen.**

Hebrews 11:1

Beauty comes in all shapes and sizes. What we describe as beautiful—or as ugly—is often in the eye of the beholder.

Consider the caterpillar. Adjectives like "beautiful" or "graceful" are seldom used to describe it. To some, this voracious eater is even "ugly." But within its soft, segmented body lies the dream of a butterfly—graceful, vibrant, stunning.

The caterpillar is an unexpected teacher. It reminds us that beauty is often hidden. What we call "ugly," God may call beautiful. What we deem insignificant might be essential to the flourishing of Earth and community.

Faith looks beyond appearances. It visualizes not just what we are but what we are becoming. As Walt Whitman rejoiced, "all is miracle."

Behold: there are hidden angels everywhere. The ugly duckling becomes the swan. The overlooked neighbor bears the Divine image. The person we dismiss or judge reveals God to eyes that are awake.

Wake me up to beauty everywhere,
O Beautiful Creator.
Let me see your beauty in all
its diverse disguises—
and even in myself.
Make me a midwife of beauty,
revealing the miracle hidden in all things.

DAY 14

Don't Be Afraid

> But the angel said to the women,
> "Do not be afraid. . . . He is not here,
> for he has been raised.
> Come, see the place where he lay.
> Then go quickly and tell his disciples,
> 'He has been raised from the dead,
> and indeed he is going ahead of you to Galilee;
> there you will see him.'"
>
> Matthew 28:5–7

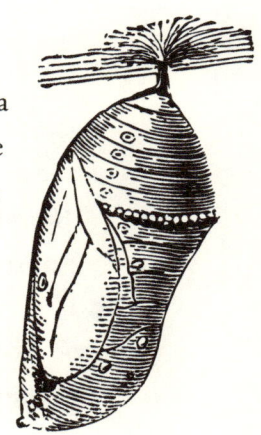

The chrysalis is the middle stage in a butterfly's metamorphosis. To the untrained eye, its stillness looks like nothing is happening. But within what resembles a tomb, a miracle unfolds: cells present in the caterpillar are transforming into legs, wings, and eyes—gathering the energy to emerge in flight.

Martin Luther once said, "In the midst of life, we are surrounded by death; and in the midst of death, we are surrounded by life."

The chrysalis is both womb and tomb. The caterpillar "dies" to become a butterfly. We, too, may need to undergo symbolic deaths—letting go of self-images, dreams, accomplishments—in order to be reborn.

The caterpillar doesn't know what it will become. If it could reflect, perhaps it would feel fear. So do we, when letting go of the past and facing the unknown. But beyond that fear lies transformation. As poet e. e. cummings wrote: "i who have died am alive again today . . . this is the birth day of life and love and wings."

Christ is risen! And so are we.

God of Creative Transformation,
I need your resurrection power.
Help me let go of what was
and trust in what can be.
In the tomb of loss,
let me find the womb of possibility—
and rise with you in joy.

DAY 15
Born to Sing

**I sing because I'm happy,
I sing because I'm free
His eye is on the sparrow,
and I know he's watching me.**

Civilla Martin

I grew up listening to Mahalia Jackson sing "His Eye Is on the Sparrow." That hymn proclaims that both people and birds sing because they're happy and because they're free—that birds reflect the joy we feel when we know we are in God's hands.

Some might consider it anthropomorphism to suggest that birds experience emotion, but a University of Wisconsin–Madison expert in birdsong notes: "When I listen to these birds sing, it seems as if they are enjoying themselves."

Birds, like humans, appear to experience both positive and negative emotional states. They may simply delight in life. They sing because they're happy—and because they're free!

Perhaps we, too, are born to sing. According to tradition, North African saint Augustine once said that when we sing, we pray twice. Singing expresses our delight in being alive in this beautiful world. Whether you're in the shower, driving your car, listening to music, or chanting—remember: you were born to sing. For God's eye is on the sparrow, and you know God is watching you with love.

Loving God,
let me live with a song in my heart.
May my words be melodies of praise
and love songs to you and all Creation.

DAY 16

Running the Race, One Step at a Time

**Forgetting what lies behind
and straining forward to what lies ahead,
I press toward the goal for the prize
of the heavenly call of God in Christ Jesus.**

Philippians 3:13–14

Aesop tells the fable of a tortoise and a hare engaged in a road race. The hare races ahead, leaving the tortoise plodding far behind. Confident of victory, the hare stops to nap, while the tortoise keeps going—slowly but steadily—and eventually wins the race.

The moral? The race of life is not always to the swift. Persistence and patience matter—in our spiritual lives and in our personal growth. With our eyes on the horizon and God's grace empowering us, we grow one step at a time and ultimately reach the finish line of love and wholeness.

What many forget is that *both* the tortoise and the hare finish the race. Some of us are swift, others methodical. Some surge forward and then rest, while others move consistently. Faithfulness to our unique personalities, gifts, and spiritual rhythms helps us experience God's presence—and live our vocation with joy.

Whether we are fast or slow, extroverted or introverted, organized or spontaneous, God is with us, luring us toward our most creative and loving selves—moment by moment, step by step.

With my eyes on the prize of your horizon,
O God, let me run—or walk—the race before me.
Help me be true to myself, using my gifts,
one faithful step at a time.

DAY 17

Welcoming Strangers

**Jesus said to his companions again,
"Peace be with you.
As the Father has sent me,
so I send you."**

John 20:21

Animal communities are often protective of their boundaries. Intrusions by other species or groups can lead to conflict. But not always.

Recently, scientists observed a remarkable mingling between two groups of Atlantic spotted dolphins (*Stenella frontalis*). Forty-six newcomers joined 120 resident dolphins. Rather than fighting, the groups dove and swam together, formed fast friendships, and likely even mated. This peaceful integration was described by scientists as a "striking" exception to typical intergroup behavior.

Boundaries matter—personal and national. Our privacy matters. But difference does not need to lead to division. We can recognize common ground (or common sea), and learn to see each other as kin.

Every stranger is a potential companion. There is no "other." We are united in the beloved community—of dolphins and humans, all Creation.

God of All Creatures,
when I am tempted to divide or exclude,
remind me that we are all connected—
joined in your energy of love and creativity.

DAY 18

Love Heals

**There is no fear in love,
but perfect love casts out fear.**

1 John 4:18

Charlie was the epitome of the childhood taunt "fraidy cat." He was the runt of the litter and was constantly picked on by the preschooler in his original home.

When we adopted him, we named him Charlie because his little mustache resembled that of the lovable tramp Charlie Chaplin. From the moment he joined our home, he was afraid—of his own shadow, of every noise he made, of everything.

But my wife Kate and I believe in love's power to heal. And we loved Charlie. And Charlie loved us back.

Each morning, before dawn, I would sit in my arts-and-crafts chair to meditate and write. Charlie would follow me, jump onto my lap, and purr softly—praying along with me, in his own way giving thanks for love and safety.

Though Charlie always remained a little anxious, the love he received allowed his spirit to grow. He found joy in yarn, paper, shafts of light, and napping on my lap.

Love heals. Charlie learned to love because he was loved. The world is healed one act, one moment, one creature at a time.

Let love be our goal as we help create, in the words of mystic Howard Thurman, "a friendly world of friendly people"—and, I would add, cats, dogs, and all of Creation.

Lover of Life, Healer of Wounds,
Companion of the Broken—
let me see your love and be your love.
Help me embrace my role
as your companion in healing the world.

DAY 19

Now Is the Only Moment There Is

**This is the day that God has made;
let us rejoice and be glad in it.**

Psalm 118:24

I'm amazed by the mayfly. After hatching, some mayfly females live only five minutes. Males might live two days. In that short time, they reproduce—starting a family of hundreds. They "live fast and die young."

Yet their lives are complete. Each mayfly fulfills its purpose.

Against the backdrop of a 13.7 billion-year-old, two-trillion-galaxy universe, we humans may seem no more significant than a mayfly. And yet, in our brief time, we can live fully, love greatly, and leave a legacy.

Every morning, I begin my day with the psalmist's words: "This is the day that God has made; I will rejoice and be glad in it." I celebrate the miracle of waking up to a new day—a day of singular, unrepeatable opportunities to do something beautiful for God and the world.

The mayfly teaches us to seize the moment with gratitude and creativity. Live this moment. Love this moment. For this very day—today—is the day that God has made.

God of time and eternity,
of change and stability,
whose care is both intimate and infinite—
show me how to live fully in this moment,
shaping the world with beauty and justice.

DAY 20

A Place to Call Home and a Person to Love

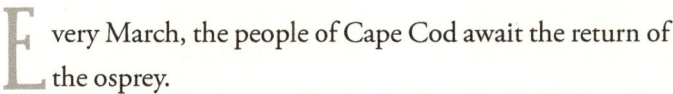

> I love thee,
> I love thee with a love
> that shall not die,
> Till the sun grows cold
> and the stars grow old.
>
> Bayard Taylor

Every March, the people of Cape Cod await the return of the osprey.

Most mornings, I would walk from South Congregational Church in Barnstable to Craigville Beach. I often met my friend John O'Connor in his Subaru, gazing out to sea, talking with God. Each March, our ritual greeting was the same: "Have you seen the osprey yet?" Then came our updates: sightings at Dowse's or Covell's Beach; the nest by the bridge. It was our shared ritual of joy.

Ospreys return to the same nests year after year, flying north from as far as Florida or Central America. Mating for life—with few exceptions—they reinhabit the nests first built by the male and refurbished each season. Scientists say the female may choose her mate based on the nest's location and quality.

In our own lives, we often choose relationships based on synchronicity and the hope of a good life. Like the osprey, we can remain faithful to our partners and to the places where we build our homes and raise our young.

A childhood hymn comes to mind: "Great Is Thy Faithfulness." That faithfulness—like the osprey's—is built into the nature of the universe.

God of Time and Space,
help me, like the osprey couple, to be faithful—
to those I love, and to the next generation.

DAY 21

I See You

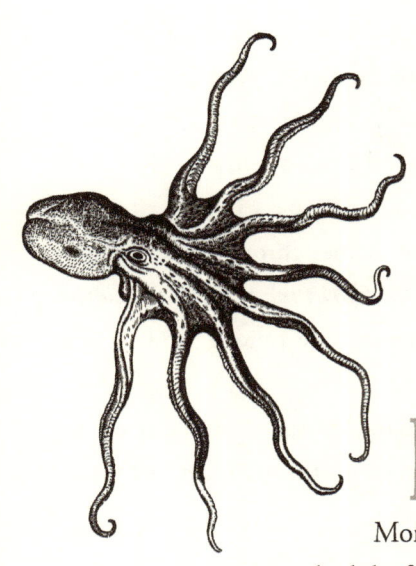

Sawubona!
"I see you!"

Zulu greeting

In her account of encounters with octopuses, Sy Montgomery writes, "I've often had the feeling that the octopus I was watching was watching me back, with an interest as keen as my own."

Alien from us in so many ways, octopuses, she notes, "represent the great mystery of the Other." Yet there are moments when, despite our differences, we truly see one another—moments when curiosity becomes connection and the unknown becomes companionship.

Among the Zulu people, greetings are not merely polite pleasantries. The traditional call-and-response—*Sawubona*, "I see you," and *Sikhona*, "I am here"—form a sacred exchange. It is a prayer of recognition: I see your mind, body, spirit, and the ancestors who walk with you. "I see you" honors the full presence and mystery of the person before me. "I am here" responds: pay attention—I matter, and so do you.

This sacred recognition echoes through many traditions: *Sawubona. Namaste. The Christ in me greets the Christ in you.* In this holy moment, we are unique, and we are connected. There is no other.

Even octopuses respond to this truth—bridging diversity not through dominance but through curiosity and mutual regard.

*Loving God, give me vision and attentiveness
to affirm "I see you" in the least and the lonely,
the bullied and the burdened,
the stranger and the friend.
Teach me that in your Beloved Community,
there are no outsiders—only kin.*

DAY 22

World-Changing Faith

> If you had faith the size of a mustard seed,
> you could say to this mulberry tree,
> "Be uprooted and planted in the sea,"
> and it would obey you.
>
> Matthew 17:6

During the summer of my seventh year, I decided to test Jesus' teaching about mustard seed faith. At Sunday school, we had just learned that even tiny faith could move mountains. So, I opened my mother's spice drawer, took a handful of mustard seeds, and planted them in her garden.

Soon, mustard plants sprang up—first one, then another. When my mother discovered them spreading, she made me cut them down: "The neighbors will complain if mustard starts growing in their yards!"

Mustard plants are contagious. One plant becomes a field of bright yellow—filling the world with beauty and providing one of the world's favorite condiments.

Small is beautiful. A small group of committed people—Jesus' followers, grassroots activists, or a teenager with autism striking for the climate—can change the world.

According to Jewish mysticism, the world is saved one person at a time. I would add: the world is transformed one moment at a time, when we dedicate ourselves to beauty, healing, reconciliation, and love.

Mustard seed faith can topple walls of injustice and shatter the glass ceilings of limitation. Have faith. And let that faith shape your life—moment by moment.

*God of Adventurous Possibility,
give me faith the size of a mustard seed
so I might move the mountains
that block abundant life for me
and for the world.*

DAY 23

Pure Joy

**God made me fast, and when I run,
I feel God's pleasure.**

Eric Liddell, *Chariots of Fire*

One of the pivotal moments in my spiritual journey came on October 15, 1970, when I learned Transcendental Meditation. That day began a journey through Christian meditation, Centering Prayer, ordination, a career in seminary and university teaching, Reiki, and the study of Jesus' healing practices.

Maharishi Mahesh Yogi, parent of TM, once said, "The natural state of humanity is joy."

In that spirit, my dog Tucker teaches me to live joyfully. When I say "walk" or "dog park," he springs to life—even from deep sleep.

Though middle-aged (seven years old), he becomes a puppy again, leaping, racing, and prancing with delight.

Joy is our natural state. Spirituality should deepen our delight in embodiment—not pull us away from it.

The pleasure of being alive: waking up, typing a sentence, shooting a basket, hugging a friend, singing a song. Feeling our skin or the skin of another.

We are created for joy. For delight. For love. And we are called to share that joy one-on-one and in community, as we seek justice and peace for all.

Joyful, joyful, we adore you—
Creator of Delight and Play.
Wake me up to the wonder of my body,
my mind, my spirit,
and the beauty of this Good Earth,
so that I may awaken joy in others.

DAY 24

The Passionate Life

> Don't ask what the world needs.
> Ask what makes you come alive,
> and go do it.
> Because what the world needs
> is people who have come alive.

Howard Thurman

My goldendoodle Tucker doesn't know how to write a book or study theology. He's never read a novel or traced the origins of the universe. But he has passion.

Every afternoon after his meal, he looks at me expectantly. If I delay, he barks—as if to say, "Now that I've eaten, let's play!" I say "pull, pull," and he grabs a toy so we can play tug-of-war.

You can see his joy, his passion—for play, for connection, for being fully seen. And passion, when shared, is contagious.

Without passion, life becomes flat and faded. Without enthusiasm, justice efforts stall. Without fire, our dreams dim.

What are *your* passions? I must confess: what you're reading reflects mine. I write because I'm passionate about sharing ideas that can bring beauty and wisdom into people's lives. I'm passionate about creating a just and healthy world for my grandchildren—and for everyone's grandchildren.

I believe that God is passionate. God creates out of love. God burns with zeal for justice, for peace, for healing. And God longs for us to live passionately, too.

*Give me, O Passionate Companion,
a holy fire for peace, beauty, love, justice,
and this Good Earth.
Let my passion join yours in healing the world
and spreading joy among all creatures.*

DAY 25

The Healing Power of Companionship

> If horses could draw, they would draw their gods as horses. The same would go for lions and oxen.
>
> Xenophanes

This ancient Greek philosopher meant his words as a critique of how humans shape gods in their own image. But they can also point to something beautiful: God comes to us as we are—where we are—with the healing presence we most need.

A personal God meets us personally. God uses people and events—and sometimes animals—to promote our well-being and spiritual growth.

Animal-assisted therapy began gaining recognition in the 1960s when child psychologist Boris Levinson noticed a breakthrough during a session with a withdrawn child. The turning point? His dog Jingles happened to be in the room. The child responded—to the dog, and then to Levinson. In his article "The Dog as a Co-Therapist," Levinson described how animals could help children heal from anxiety, depression, and even schizophrenia.

After the school shooting in Uvalde, Texas, ten Golden Retrievers were sent to greet returning students. According to Bonnie Fear, crisis response coordinator for the Lutheran Church Charities K-9 Comfort Dog Ministry,

> "There was a lot of hesitancy and anxiety about getting out of the car and going into the school. So we placed the dogs outside, and I do believe that did help some of the kids see the dog and go, "OK, well, I'm going to go pet the dog."

The gift is simple: presence. Calm, loving presence. No judgment. No expectation. Just love. That's what heals.

Healing God,
make me an instrument of your peace.
Help me offer calm, loving presence
to wounded souls—human
and other-than-human.

DAY 26
A Sensational Life

The monk ought to be as the Cherubim and the Seraphim— all eye.

Abba Bessarion,
fourth-century North African Desert Father

When my grandsons were small, I bought them a stuffed hammerhead shark we called "Hammy." He quickly became the star of their make-believe games, sparked hours of shark documentaries, and captured their imaginations.

No one knows the exact purpose of the hammerhead's distinctive shape, but its wide head grants it 360-degree vision—allowing it to see above and below at all times. Its unusual form increases sensory perception, acting much like a living antenna.

Like the monk, the hammerhead is not only all eye—it is all sense, fully attuned to its surroundings in pursuit of sustenance and survival.

The hammerhead teaches us to stay alert to the world. Spirituality deepens not only through inward stillness but also through sensory engagement. We can withdraw from the senses in meditation, yes—but we also meet God through the senses, which mystics describe as portals to the Divine.

As Saint Bonaventure wrote, the physical universe is a "vestige" of God—a trace of the Word made flesh. The hammerhead invites us to awaken—to become all eye, all ear, all wonder.

Open my senses, O Beauty Maker,
that I may taste and see your goodness,
smell the perfume of your presence,
see your face in all Creation,
touch holiness in every body,
and hear heaven and Nature sing.

DAY 27

Rise Up!

**Those who wait for the Lord
shall renew their strength;
they shall mount up with wings like eagles;
they shall run and not be weary;
they shall walk and not faint.**

Isaiah 40:31

"Still I rise," proclaims Maya Angelou, celebrating the power, resilience, and creativity of African American women in a world that constantly questions their dignity and worth. The human spirit must not be confined by racism or sexism. When inspired, set free, it rises—radiant, and unbound.

Eagles rise. They soar to far horizons, fix their gaze on what matters, and refuse to be limited by obstacles. Though grounded in reality, they do not let it confine them. Their flight is an act of imagination.

So it is with us. Within the limitations of our histories, challenges, and context, new adventures are born. Concrete realities can be the womb of possibility. From the heights to which eagles soar, we envision new worlds—communities of peace, children laughing across racial lines, societies shaped by justice and joy.

We cannot rise alone. We rise with companions—with those who, as poet and activist June Jordan wrote, become "the ones we have been waiting for." Together, with the eagles and the freedom-seekers, we rise.

*God of possibility,
whose imaginative love breaks every barrier,
give me persistence, resilience,
courage, and vision. Help me rise—
and help me lift others as I rise.*

DAY 28

Listen as Well as Speak

**Francis of Assisi carefully exhorted all birds,
all animals, all reptiles, and also
insensible creatures
to love and praise their Creator...
daily observing their obedience
in his own experience.**

Thomas of Celano, *The Life of St. Francis*

According to Saint Francis's biographer, Thomas of Celano, the birds once chirped so loudly during one of Francis's sermons that no one could hear his message. He turned to them and said, "My sister swallows, now it is time for me also to speak. Listen to the word of the Lord and stay quiet."

To everyone's amazement, the birds hushed—completely still—until Francis finished preaching.

In the spirit of Pentecost, the swallows heard in their own language. And they listened.

Their example reminds us: we are called not only to sing praise, but also to listen—to God, to others, to the deep wisdom around us.

Too often, we're stuck in transmission mode—telling others what God is saying, what they should do, what's right. But God's voice also comes in silence, in events, in sighs too deep for words.

We must listen before we speak. Listen before advising. Listen for the voice of the Divine in our companions, in our hearts, and in the cries of the world.

Like the birds of the air,
let me listen as well as sing.
Let me pause to hear your still, small voice—
and let that voice guide my words,
so that all I speak reflects your wisdom and love.

DAY 29

Rise and Shine

Look to this day:
For it is life, the very life of life. . . .
Look well therefore to this day;
Such is the salutation to the ever-new dawn!

Kalidasa

At 4:30 a.m., my dog Tucker is already at my side—panting, brushing against me as I rise from bed. Now that I'm in my seventies, getting up is a bit more wobbly than it used to be—and Tucker, my 95-pound goldendoodle, doesn't make it any easier.

But in his eyes, there is joy. Expectancy. "It's a new day," he seems to say. "Let's rise and shine. There are adventures ahead!"

He embodies the wisdom of Kalidasa, the Hindu poet and playwright:

Look to this day. . . . For it is the very life of life.

No day will ever be quite like today.

How we start the day matters. Our attitude shapes what follows. For Tucker, the day begins with water, a trip outside, a biscuit—and then curling up beside me as I meditate and write. His presence reminds me that each day is full of possibility. The plans I made may change. Surprises may arise. But if I meet the day with expectancy, the world opens its arms.

*God of the New Day,
help me greet this day
with wonder and welcome.
Let me live each moment as a sacred gift—
your invitation to adventure, to love, to create.*

DAY 30

For God's Sake, Use Your Brain!

> You shall love the Lord your God
> with all your heart, and with all your soul,
> and with all your mind.
>
> Matthew 22:37–38

There is a continuity of experience that connects humanity with all living things. Some form of intelligence may permeate the cosmos, flowing through every being, guiding movements and decisions—whether consciously or not. Perhaps the universe is the reflection of the Mind of God. Just as science has revealed that the human mind is distributed throughout the body, Divine intelligence may be distributed throughout all of Creation.

Consider the crow. Despite being part of a group known (unfortunately) as a "murder," crows are as intelligent as young children.

Scientists have found that crows can:

- solve puzzles
- use and make tools
- bend wire
- cooperate
- hold grudges
- remember human kindness
- communicate about individual humans
- and even mourn their dead.

Their brains are proportionately the same size as humans—and they may use them more efficiently than we do. "Bird brain" might not be an insult after all.

Crows challenge us to use our minds, to solve problems creatively, to become thinkers and learners. They fulfill their vocation by being fully themselves—and so must we.

Imaginative and innovative God,
help me use my mind for your glory—
to do good, to create beauty,
and to make this Good Earth
a better home for all.

DAY 31

Strength in Stillness

> Be still, and know that I am God!
> The Lord of hosts is with us;
> the God of Jacob is our refuge.
>
> Psalm 46:10–11

During the summer of 2020, at the height of the COVID pandemic, Artichoke the Pangolin became a spirit friend for my two grandchildren, then ten and eight. Kate and I bought them stuffed animals to cuddle and play with, and together we wrote stories about Artichoke's adventures on Cape Cod.

Imagine a pangolin as a spirit animal! You may not even have heard of pangolins—the world's only scaled mammals. They're endangered due to the belief that their scales have medicinal and magical properties.

The word *pangolin* is derived from the Malay word *penggulung*, meaning "roller." When threatened, pangolins roll into a tight ball to protect themselves from predators. Even lions may bat at a rolled-up pangolin like a volleyball, but they can't get inside. A mother pangolin will also curl around her baby for comfort and safety.

In times of danger, the pangolin goes inward. While we eventually must respond to the world's challenges, there are times we need to do the same—retreat inward, minimize stress, and find the quiet center where spiritual resilience is born.

In times of stress,
God of Peace and Resilience,
help me roll up and find the quiet center—
so that I may spring forward in
acts of kindness and justice.

DAY 32

Everyone Matters

**No one is too small
to make a difference.**

Greta Thunberg

In *Celtic Saints and Their Animal Friends* (Anamchara Books), Edward Sellner tells of the unique relationship between Saint Colman mac Duagh (560–632) and his companion animals. A fly would walk up and down the lines of his manuscript as he read, keeping his place. If Colman was called away, the fly would sit on the last line until he returned. A mouse helped keep him awake to fulfill his monastic vows, and a rooster crowed each morning to ensure he rose for prayer.

Even the smallest creature can play a vital role. The world is saved one being at a time. Each person—regardless of age, gender, physical condition, or neurodiversity—can tip the scales from despair to healing.

In my ministry, I often told children: "You matter. You can do great things." It's still true, for grown-ups as well as children. Your devotion—unseen though it may be—can shift the world toward justice, beauty, and healing.

*God of the micro and the macro,
help me recognize your presence
in the sacrament of the present moment—
and dedicate each action to the healing
of my companions and this Good Earth.*

DAY 33

Deep Intuition

**Then Jacob woke from his sleep and said,
"Surely the Lord is in this place—
and I did not know it!"**

Genesis 28:17

Throughout my life, I've shared space with many dogs: Duke, Ed, Flaca, Freddie, Chelsea, and now Tucker—who's curled up beside me as I write. Sometimes I simply *think* about taking a walk, and there's Tucker—panting, prancing, ready to go. He may not only sense time and movement; he might read my thoughts. Our companionship runs deep, shaped by patterns, energy, and presence.

Tucker reminds me that the world is full of quiet knowing. We're often too distracted to notice—but deep down, we are all mystics. Like Jacob, we may wake from spiritual sleep and discover ladders of angels connecting us to heaven.

Every moment holds potential. For Tucker, the world is full of adventures, treats, and wonder. Through him, I'm reminded: "God is in this place—and I can know it."

*God of Dreams and Wakefulness,
train my senses to notice
your movements and the hearts
of those around me.
Help me live in harmony with you
and all Creation.*

DAY 34

The Race Is to the Slow

In the morning, while it was still very dark, Jesus got up and went out to a deserted place, and there he prayed.

Mark 1:35

In *The Hidden Life of Trees*, Peter Wohlleben shares that young trees thrive when their growth is slowed by the shade of older trees. Slow, steady growth increases longevity and resilience. Jesus knew this truth. He didn't rush into his ministry. He paused, prayed, and listened.

But today's culture worships speed. We push children to excel too early. We rage at slow internet. We rush through our days—and sometimes, our prayers.

So I've chosen to see delays as spiritual practice. When waiting in line or logging onto my computer, I pause. I breathe. I pray for those around me. I fill my soul with sacred stillness.

Slowness can bring clarity. Trees grow slowly—and become strong. Jesus paused—and found direction.

Slow my pace, God of Time and Eternity.
Let me pause and awaken
to your energy flowing through me.
Help me walk with grace and intention.

DAY 35

Breathe Deeply and Rest in God

> Jesus said to them again,
> "Peace be with you.
> As the Father has sent me, so I send you."
> When he had said this,
> he breathed on them and said,
> "Receive the Holy Spirit."
>
> John 20:21–22

My wife sometimes calls me a "tree-hugging hippie." I accept the label with gratitude. I love trees. Their shapes, their stillness, the light filtering through their leaves—each season teaches something sacred.

In winter, trees rest. They let go of what no longer serves them. They stop working so hard. They even detox. Peter Wohlleben tells us that tightly packed soil can cause a tree to sicken because it cannot breathe.

The same is true for us. When we're packed too tightly by stress, we can't thrive. We need loose soil. Space. Stillness. Breath.

Like trees, we must exhale, rest, and renew. Spiritual rest heals our nervous systems and rewires our spirits. Deep breathing is holy.

Breathe in me, Breath of God.
Fill me with life and peace.
Let me rest in your love
and awaken renewed.

DAY 36
Healing Spirit

**The wound is the place
where the Light enters you.**

Rumi

Alfred North Whitehead claimed the universe aims toward beauty. I believe it also aims toward health and justice. As Mother Teresa said, "There is a light in this world, a healing spirit more powerful than any darkness we may face."

Our animal companions testify to this healing spirit. Ants can be trained to detect breast cancer. Dogs can predict seizures, alert diabetics to low blood sugar, and identify cancer with extraordinary accuracy. Fruit flies, pigeons, and rats also detect disease.

Healing is all around us. And like animals, we are called to be healers. As Marianne Williamson says, "Each of us has a unique part to play in the healing of the world."

Empathy is sacred. Let us be mystics and healers—one act at a time.

Empathic God,
awaken my heart to the pain
and joy around me.
Inspire me to be a vessel
of healing and wholeness.

DAY 37
Elephant Whisperers

**And the elephant sings
deep in the forest-maze.**

Ted Hughes

The poet John Donne called the elephant "nature's greatest masterpiece." Elephants are empathetic, collaborative, joyful, and wise. They grieve. They play. They bond across boundaries—and even form friendships with humans.

The film *The Elephant Whisperers* tells the story of Raghu, an orphaned elephant raised by Bomman and Belli of the Kattunayakan tribe. Their love saved him—and Raghu returned their love with affection and trust.

There are no boundaries love cannot cross. No creature too alien to connect. Hospitality, compassion, and healing arise when we choose love over fear.

Loving God,
teach me to love like the elephant—
to embrace difference,
to cross boundaries,
and to grow in compassion.

DAY 38

Touch Transforms

Jesus came and took her by the hand and lifted her up. Then the fever left her.

Mark 1:30–31

Two male North Atlantic right whales were observed swimming side by side, fins gently draped over one another. "Are they hugging?" the scientist wondered. "Are they showing love?"

Their grace, their gentleness, their bond—it was like watching a slow waltz. A heartbeat of hope.

Touch heals. For infants and adults alike, physical contact reduces stress, boosts immunity, and promotes emotional well-being.

As a Reiki Healing Touch master, I know touch balances energy and brings peace. Welcomed, loving touch helps us flourish.

Jesus healed with a touch. So can we.

Touch me, Healing God,
that I may offer your healing touch to others—
bringing peace, wholeness, and justice
to this Good Earth.

DAY 39

Tasting and Smelling the Goodness of Creation

O taste and see that the Lord is good; happy are those who take refuge in him.

Psalm 34:8

In *The Soul of the Octopus*, Sy Montgomery describes how octopuses taste through their entire bodies—especially through their suckers. They recognize people, form attachments, and remember affection. Each time Montgomery visited Octavia, a two-year-old octopus, she came to the top of the tank to greet Montgomery. She wanted to *taste* Montgomery—to know her.

God meets us in the senses. In color and scent. In touch and sound. In dreams and intuitions. The whole body becomes a cathedral.

Taste and see. Inhale the sacred. Touch the mystery.

God of Sensory Wonder,
awaken my body to your presence
in every breath and every encounter.

DAY 40
The Phoenix

**i who have died
am alive again today.**

e. e. cummings

No creature is like the phoenix—mythical, yes, but deeply true. From ashes it rises. From death, new life emerges. It is a metaphor for a profound reality.

In this time of crisis—of forest fires, melting glaciers, rising seas—we need phoenixes. We need to become resurrection people, bearers of hope, builders of new life.

We are, as June Jordan says, "the ones we've been waiting for." Let us rise—not only for ourselves, but for future generations and all our animal kin.

God of Resurrection Love,
let us rise with the phoenix—
and with us, renew all Creation.

CONCLUSION

The Pilgrimage Continues: Running with the Elephants

The ancient story of the blindfolded seekers and the elephant reminds us that each of us perceives only a part of the Divine mystery. One touches the tail and calls it a rope. Another feels the ear and calls it a fan. Each describes a truth—but none the whole.

For the living elephant doesn't stand still. It breathes, moves, mourns, and dances. To know it fully, we must move with it—watch, listen, run to keep up.

So it is with God. Our spiritual journey is an unfolding encounter. A living elephant. A living God.

God comes to us in sacred texts and teachers—in Jesus, in the prophets, in the mystics of every tradition. But also in dogs and whales, in thunder and pine trees, in laughter and grief, in the color purple.

Creation is the first scripture. Every creature praises. Every life reveals Divine wisdom. Every moment can be a sacrament.

Let us run with the elephants. Let us honor every life, protect the Earth, and live together as kin—companions, healers, and lovers of the world.

Namaste.
The Spirit in me greets the Spirit in you.
Let us walk—and run—
this sacred Earth together.

More inspiration from
Bruce G. Epperly...

God Online
A Mystic's Guide to the Internet

Perhaps the world is saved one act, one click, or one post at a time.

When we do ordinary things with great love, as Therese of Lisieux counseled, we bring beauty and healing to our companions on the Internet and to the planetary mind. The omnipresent God is as near as the next key stroke, the next post or response to another's online comment. We need a whole-person spirituality grounded in a sense of the holiness of all creation and reverence for life, despite the conflicts that characterize our world—and given the amount of time most of us spend online, we need to include these activities in our spiritual lives.

Bruce Epperly guides his spiritual Internet manual with the wisdom of the Christian mystical tradition. These insights, both ancient and modern, help us to claim our vocation as God's companions in healing the world—through the vehicle of social media and other online interactions. Each chapter's dialogue with a mystic concludes with a spiritual practice that enables us to discover, in the spirit of the patriarch Jacob's exclamation, that "God is online, and we did not know it."

Become Fire!
Guideposts for Interspiritual Pilgrims

In the spirit of God's call to creative transformation, Bruce Epperly invites you to join him on a holy adventure in spiritual growth, inspired by the evolving wisdom of Christianity and the world's great spiritual traditions, innovative global spiritual practices, and emerging visions of reality. Epperly explores the many resources of Christian spirituality in dialogue with the spiritual practices of the world's great wisdom traditions, describing the gifts other spiritual paths contribute to the pathway of Jesus; at the same time, he uses the lens of the spiritual practices Jesus has inspired throughout Christian history to examine these spiritual paths.

Epperly write as a Christian committed to Jesus, whose teachings and way of life he believes lead to pathways of healing and creative personal and planetary transformation. By embracing the diverse insights of spiritual wisdom givers, physicists, cosmologists, healing practitioners, and Earth keepers, we can meet the Earth's current challenges with love, joy, and a united strength.

Jesus
Mystic, Healer, and Prophet

Who do you say Jesus is?

In his answer to this age-old question, Bruce Epperly brings us a new vision of Jesus of Nazareth, the healer, mystic, and prophet who is always more than we can imagine. This Jesus embraces all times and places with his mystical union with God, his healing presence, and his transforming prophetic challenge.

Rather than requiring supernatural intervention from outside our reality, the Jesus of the Gospels is present in the natural, ordinary-yet-amazing world we too inhabit. The energy of his love opens up new realms of unexpected possibilities within our daily lives. At the same time, he points the way to meeting the challenges of our broken world. He calls us to venture out beyond the safe boundaries of doctrines and institutions, into new adventures of spiritual growth and inclusive ethical imagination. The quest to know Jesus never ends—and yet at the same time, he lives in us, inspiring us to embrace the ever-present God and transform the world.

Homegrown Mystics
Restoring Our Nation with the Healing Wisdom of America's Visionaries

These days, politicians, preachers, and ordinary citizens alike speak of healing the soul of America. If the United States is to survive and flourish, the nation must reclaim a common spirit and calm the voices of hate and incivility. This is a spiritual task, taking us beyond the parochialism of creed, political party, and belief systems to affirm our essential oneness as humans and Americans.

"In his first inaugural address, Lincoln implored his fellow citizens to awaken and embrace the better angels of their nature. In our own troubled times, we desperately need to do likewise. Bruce Epperly's beautiful book can help us do precisely that. His profiles of thirteen people whose spirituality reflects the best of the American tradition are both informative and inspirational. We all need role models to help us be better people and worthier citizens—Epperly's thirteen admirably serve that purpose."

— Kerry Walters, priest and author of *Blessed Peacemakers* and *Let Justice Be Done*

BRUCE G. EPPERLY has served as a seminary professor and administrator, university chaplain, and congregational pastor. An ordained minister with the United Church of Christ and Christian Church (Disciples of Christ), he is the author of more than sixty books, including *From Cosmos to Cradle: Meditations on the Incarnation* and *The Elephant Is Running: Process and Open and Relational Theology and Religious Pluralism.*

AnamcharaBooks.com

www.ingramcontent.com/pod-product-compliance
Lightning Source LLC
Chambersburg PA
CBHW060529080526
44586CB00012B/678